For Matthew, Bryan, Eva, and Robert.

"The future ain't what it used to be."
Yogi Berra

THE NOSTRADAMUS CODE:

WORLD WAR III
2006-2012

by
Michael Rathford

ISBN 0-9776341-0-8

First printing • 500 Copies • December 5

Truth Revealed
PUBLISHING

4940 Merrick Rd, #262
Massapequa Park, NY 11762
1-516-584-2775

Printed in the U.S.A. by
Morris Publishing
2 East Highway 30
Kearney, NE 47
1-800-650-7888

TABLE OF CONTENTS

Devastating accidental weaponry explosions from earth tumult

Ruptured earth energy fields cause meteorite storm

Research into warping time leads to disaster

The weapons of WWWIII

New, horrific, secret, radical weapons monstrosities in WWW III

ETW unleashed on San Andreas and New Madrid faults

Antichrist obtains ETW through espionage, bribery, treachery

Death by radio waves

Eugenics

Human eugenics research advanced by the King of Terror

Eugenics scientists meet grisly deaths from public backlash

Part VII: The geological and spiritual earth shift...................................64

Part I: Introduction

1.1. Nostradamus and his "quatrains"

Nostradamus was a physician and prophet of the 16th century living in France at the time of the Inquisition. He was recognized as a brilliant physician who knew effective measures against the plague victims of the time, a rarity in his profession. Nostradamus as a seer wrote about "quatrains", or four line poems, about his visions collected over his lifetime. The quatrains are enveloped in deeply obscure, twisted, nested symbolism and encryptions (such as anagrams, different languages, etc.) that is virtually impossible to untangle by a casual observer. Perhaps the greatest difficulty was that he intentionally scrambled them in terms of their historical order.

Quatrains I have found particularly evocative and masterful in symbolism and interpretation, and serve as examples of Nostradamus' intents and talents, are, Centurie III, Quatrain 13, microchips and electricity, Centurie IV, Quatrain 29, the dichotomy of technology vs. spirituality in the 20th century, and Centurie II, Quatrain 75, a plane lands on the deck of an aircraft carrier in a pivotal moment of WWWIII.

1.2. How did Nostradamus do it?

Nostradamus was born with an inner "sixth sense", i.e. a strong intuition and great psychic abilities. Secondly he had enormous drive to develop it. His grandfather apparently passed him books on witchcraft that allowed him to experiment with some rituals. He also had access to "lost" manuscripts handed down outside of the libraries of the time. He talks about guides from the astral plane and from other worlds who helped him. Some pointed him in the direction of esoteric plant recipes and mind-enhancing drugs (but he emphasized they only enhanced his powers and were not the source of them). One apparently bestowed on him a mirror during one of his meditations. The mirror was especially important to his predictions.

Nostradamus also talked of using different crystals to focus on various telepathic frequencies. Occasionally he refers to staring at fire or water (such as in a bowl on a tripod) as a way of focusing his mind. He had access to some lost works of mysticism from his travels (apparently to some Moslem lands). He communicated with other expert astrologers and mystical teachers. However it is possible that some of his notes about and explanations of his techniques were a means of throwing the Inquisition off track.

One of the most amazing possibilities explored was that in a sort of "twist of time" Nostradamus was tapping into the subconscious of the people from the future who contacted him.

Some have wondered about Nostradamus' healing capabilities. He talks about a sort of holistic approach to health and reveals that he was skillful in avoiding the shock that was induced in many patients of surgeons at the time using psychic approaches. He talked about the importance of the "aura" of the person in determining the health of the patient and criticized the practice of treating symptoms. He said that a patient will find some other way to make themselves sick if their critical mental attitude is awry. He talked about cancer being caused by deeply ingrained self-sabotaging thoughts. Nostradamus also confirmed what many have speculated, that he was able to see future approaches to treating the diseases he encountered (such as the plague) and adopt key aspects of the techniques.

1.3. "Simultaneous Time"

"Simultaneous time" is a difficult concept that refers to the illusion of earthly time seen from higher spiritual planes. Between lives, the soul has the capability to review lifetimes free of the constraints of time. This state of consciousness is also achieved in hypno-regression subjects who are highly "somnambulistic", i.e. conducive to deep trance states. They can review not only past lifetimes but future ones. But beyond this, it is as if they are actually living them at the moment they describe them. So, for example, the student of Nostradamus that Dr. Rathford regressed would see himself and Nostradamus as actually living, and Nostradamus would be communicating directly from his own time to ours as a living person.

1.4. Ways to view Nostradamus and the prophecies

A scathing work of criticism and ridicule has been leveled at Nostradamus by the famous "debunker", James Randi. Nevertheless, buried in the unparalleled close-mindedness and vitriol, Randi makes some reasonable points, the most damning of which, reiterated by the skeptics through the centuries, is that Nostradamus' "predictions" are veiled in such obscure symbolism that they could mean anything, and that interpretations are impossible in the absence of precision in language. He has a very valid point.

But the works of Dr. Michael Rathford give us a renewed, fresh perspective into the matter. Not only are the past predictions laid bare, but so are all the future ones. This book gives a very *precise* vision of the future, with a rigor bordering on the quality of even scientific papers (which themselves contain speculation and a lack of confidence and absolute specificity at times). Perhaps the skeptics can argue that the "fulfillment" of all his prior prophecies were merely due to the creative interpretations or vivid imaginations of enthusiastic supporters. But they will not be able to deny the reality of these explicit visions as (or "if", as the case may be) it unfolds before them.

However, the ultimate measure of Nostradamus' true talents will be revealed shortly for us all to personally witness and attest to the presence or lack thereof. And even if one ignores the Nostradamus aspect, leaving aside for a moment the question of the "source" of the predictions, this book contains a treasure trove of specific predictions about our near future. Here is something that is not buried in mysticism or obscurity and is open to any one who has an open mind.

1.5. Free will vs. Fatalism

Nostradamus' preponderance of bleak and horrid prophecies sometimes has the effect of causing people to adopt an attitude of resigned nihilism or fatalism. "What's the use?" But this is precisely the mental attitude that he was fervently attacking. The earth history-flow has a kind of "inertia" that he learned to read through his highly refined and developed mental concentration. If we continue on our present path, i.e. the "course of least resistance", the worst of the horrible, apocalyptic visions will be realized. But through focused thought and determination the most severe scenarios can be avoided.

Nostradamus repeatedly emphasizes the urgency of his mission and his frustration with man's apathy in the face of his predictions. His psychic abilities were so profound and developed that had he lived in other times he might have been revered almost as a God, but in the Inquisition his talent was wasted. Nostradamus was something like a psychoanalyst for the entire human race, and was quite frustrated with his patient's continual tendency to sabotage and destroy himself in spite of the doctor's--literally--divinely inspired advice.

Another interesting theme is that Nostradamus seems to indicate that the Antichrist is the embodiment of all evil in mankind since the time of creation. In other words, our own evil thoughts and deeds contribute indirectly and directly to the terrible crescendo his horrible nature. The grisly earthly drama with him in the starring role, foretold for centuries as far back as the Old Testament of the Bible, is actually a lesson of the highest order for us to clean our own mental and bodily temples of the encrusted pollution of ages. The awesome power of our own thoughts will confront us face to face. Just as the atrocities and genocide that Hitler perpetrated under the name of the Reich are the logical conclusion of insane fascism, racism, intolerance, and imperialism, the shrieking crescendo of WWWIII is the embodiment of all our hidden and concealed crimes against our fellow humans.

I would like to bring out an example of the importance and interpretation that should be attributed to Nostradamus' prophecies. In Centurie VI, Quatrain 34 he correctly foresees the Challenger shuttle disaster. But in his interpretation, he also indicates that NASA would cover-up the source of failure and not reveal it to the general public. This arguably occurred, but because of the dynamic efforts of one man in particular *outside* of NASA, the truth of the disaster has probably in fact been revealed.

The man is the eminent physicist Richard Feynman, who wrote about his experience on the Challenger investigation committee in his book, "What do you care what other people think, Mr. Feynman?" Throughout his great work one can see very directly the efforts of NASA administrators to put up a smokescreen to the public and defy his determined, heroic efforts to find the truth. Did he indeed thwart one of Nostradamus' many uncanny and depressing predictions? Can this be regarded as a case of the power of an individual to defy the smothering inertia of foretold negativity? Of the power of each one of use to untangle and defy secret conspiracies, and those who derive their power through the concealment of truth, and greedily, madly clutch it?

Nostradamus refers to many different dark secrets of our times, ranging from the Cabal that manipulates the world economy and military conflicts to the unspeakably horrible secret military weapon researches. Are we to assert that we have no influence over those who attempt to conceal truth from us? Or would the world be a far better place if we all had the dogged determination and curiosity that Feynman embodied? The courage to defy and transcend people who say "you don't know what you're doing and you have no place in this matter"? Or not be bludgeoned into silent submission by keywords like "matter of national security"? as our governments develop the most grisly weapons of destruction ever conceived in the history of (in)humanity?

Nostradamus' underlying, "golden" message is that every individual contributes to the flow of history, that free will exists and can avert disaster through sensible use--but apathy is perhaps the most negative and lethal contribution of all.

"There is free will. He wants you to know about them so the worse effects can be avoided."

"Nostradamus believed, as I do, in the theory of `probable futures', of nexus on the lines of time with many possible courses branching off in all directions. He believed that if man had the knowledge he could see which time line his future was headed down and reverse it before it was too late."

Part II: Cast and Characters of the Time of Troubles

The Antichrist

2.1. Background/overview of the Antichrist
2.2. Political/religious philosophies of the Antichrist

Ogmios

2.3. The Celtic legend of the great orator

The Popes and the Catholic Church

2.4. Death of the three popes / Catholic Church & the Antichrist
2.5. Assassination of the current pope
2.6. Second-to-last pope "swallowed" by Antichrist's scheming
2.7. The treachery of the final pope
2.8. Demise of the Catholic Church

The Cabal and secret conspiracies

2.9. Cabal's teeth in the international power flow
2.10. Cabal involved in military and economic conquests
2.11. Cabal destroyed by the Antichrist
2.12. Fundamentalist fanatics' infiltrations into governments
2.13. Manipulation of the IRA in Ireland by the underworld
2.14. Wealthy U.S. businessman a closet revolutionary and Nazi

General international political climate

2.14. Fundamentalist censorship
2.15. Terrorist assassinations

2.1. Background/overview of the Antichrist

(Centurie I, Quatrain 76)

The Antichrist made a promise to himself to rule the world in a past incarnation and the wheel of karma has turned to give him the opportunity in this lifetime. His potential and opportunities for evil will be counterbalanced by the ability to do well. In early 0s he is beginning the realization of his ambitions, and will start his political career at a local level and keep advancing, becoming ever greedier of power.

The Antichrist will become a world leader even though he misuses his power. The root meanings of his names will give a clue of his destiny and what he is capable of. The name may sound somewhat barbaric to European ears. He will be influenced by old customs known in the literature but generally forgotten.

The Antichrist will be worse than Hitler. In ~9 he's living in the Middle East. He is at a very crucial time in his life, when impressions will influence his future life path. Currently in the realm there is a lot of violence, political maneuvering, and corruption. The atmosphere is having an effect an effect on him and he's coming to realize what his destiny is.

(Centurie VIII, Quatrain 77)

He will succeed in conquests but only at the cost of terrible bloodshed by conventional weapons, but will save his nuclear arsenal for later unspeakable deeds. So many people will be killed that the living will not be able to haul them away to be buried fast enough. The people of the world will be accustomed to the sight of corpses and the sight of death will not make people squeamish because they will be around it so much.

Neither Kadaffi or the Ayatollah Khomeni are the Antichrist, but they will contribute to the destabilization of the region that will aid his rise to power.

He will be educated in Egypt because of its current stability and strategic position to the Middle East and North Africa.

The social upheavals of the times will contribute to laying the way open for the Antichrist to take over. Various countries will have their social and political structure will be turned totally upside down. Religious fanatics (not spiritual people) will come into power and believe they are justified in their draconian campaigns. The religious fervor allows the Antichrist to come into power through persuasive guile. His followers will regard him as a religious figure.

(Centurie X, Quatrain 71)

Despite the massive propaganda campaigns of the Antichrist that paint a grand and wondrous picture of his worldwide achievements, other glimpses of his heinous atrocities "behind the scenes" will leak out. He will not be able to live up to the image his followers project of him.

(Centurie I, Quatrain 50)

The Antichrist will be in action near the Mediterranean Sea, the Red Sea, and the Arabian Sea. He will gain immense world-wide power. Thursday will be an important day for him; he will take it as his day of worship. He will be a threat to everyone but particularly in the East because he will control both China and Russia and the entire Asian continent under his control, for the first time in world history.

(Centurie I, Quatrain 55)

The social and political upheavals orchestrated by the Antichrist will be felt particularly in northern, developed countries with cooler climates. During his time societies will be torn and cast into chaos and confusion. Many doomsayers will arise as false prophets, claiming to have divine revelations and know the path of salvation for the people.

(Centurie I, Quatrain 92)

For a short period the reign of the Antichrist over his realm will be no fighting because of his police state. But people will begin to rebel in the memory of lost freedoms. There will be very much death and destruction, with many people dying for their cause. Prophecies from the Revelations will apply, such as the quote about "rivers of blood up to horse's harnesses". The times will be extremely violent and traumatic.

(Centurie I, Quatrain 80)

The Antichrist will take Thursday as his day of reverence. There will be enormous warfare and bloodshed from his weapons, one "a monster borne of a very hideous beast". Hard radiation will cause gross deformities, terrible mutations in nature, in plants and animals as well as Mother Earth. In the period 7 or 1 there will be great pain and despair.

2.2. Political & religious philosophies of the Antichrist

(Centurie X, Quatrain 75)

The Antichrist will develop a systematic philosophy based on Marx and Engels that takes advantage of the elements related to the complete control of a population. Russia and China will be vulnerable to the philosophy because of the past receptivity to Communism. The Antichrist will use his philosophy as a way of conquering the entire Asian continent before setting out to take over the rest of the world. His philosophies will be propagated through manipulations of the different institutions of political power.

(Centurie III, Quatrain 95)

The Antichrist will corrupt the religion of Christianity with the intent of destroying it, but also distort the beliefs of Islam. He will disguise his agenda of conquest as a way of life and a replacement for religion.

(Centurie III, Quatrain 19)

The Antichrist will study and emulate Hitler and his techniques avidly to try to surpass him and avoid his mistakes. He will have access to books and material not available or known to the general public. It will be possible for him to obtain secret Nazi documents on Hitler and he will study them very carefully.

The Antichrist will be doomed from the start of his campaign, because he is against central spiritual forces that make up the fabric of the universe. For people who choose this path, "It's just a matter of how far they go before they fail and what effects they have on the lives around them." Like the ultimate downfall of many tyrants his empire and power will be inherently unstable. His own sub commanders will be power hungry in his image and his authority will fragment around him. The political map of the world, the boundaries of countries, will change but the continents of the world will still be shaped the same.

2.3. Ogmios

Ogmios is the counterforce to the Antichrist who will help tear down the tyranny and balance the universe in a way that is harmonious to man's central spiritual source. He will be supported by many countries still fighting the Antichrist. He will probably arise from the underground movement. In one of the countries conquered by the Antichrist the underground will be tightly organized. Ogmios will arise from it, and confront the

Antichrist in the area in Eurasia close to Constantinople, as WWWIII is approaching its end. Ogmios wil come from somewhere in central Europe. He is very well prepared spiritually for the task, because his opponent is very powerful with a strong aura of negative powers.

Ogmios will be "of the people". He will have worked up through the ranks from a simple background, attaining his accomplishments through honest work. He will have technical training but will rely mainly on his practicality. He's an old soul who has his priorities straight and can see the root of matters. He is one who will help pave the way for the "Great Genius". Ogmios realizes he is not the one to lead the world to ultimate peace, but he is the one to help bring down "the one who would destroy the world" (the Antichrist) to open the way for the one who will guide the world to ultimate peace.

(Centurie V, Quatrain 24)

The organization run by Ogmios will survive the worst of the time of troubles and will serve the basis for future governments after the Antichrist is put down. The "glory of the sun" is behind Ogmios; is a man of great stature, but has a direct, sometimes "gruff" personality. He makes a good friend but a terrible enemy. He will be an upstanding man of strong principles and morals, making him a strong adversary to the Antichrist. His principles are his own and not influenced by dogma, and his organization under his leadership is the effective opposition to the Antichrist, but he is not haughty.

(Centurie II, Quatrain 85)

Ogmios will be "small" in that his forces and resources are meager. His underground movement will be scraping to keep body and soul together.

Ogmios is the Celtic equivalent of Hercules. He is represented as an old, bald-headed man with wrinkled and sun-burnt skin yet possessing the attributes of Hercules. He draws a multitude of joyful followers and admirers by beautiful chains of gold and amber attached to their ears. The other end of the chains is fixed to his tongue, and he bestows on his captives a smiling face. This is the native god of eloquence, regarded with the reverence given to Hercules, because he had accomplished his feats through glorious speech. His speech shows itself best in his old age. The chains indicate the bond between the orator's tongue and the ears of enraptured listeners.

2.4. Death of the three popes / Catholic Church & the Antichrist

(Centurie IV, Quatrain 86)

The present pope will be assassinated and the next pope will not last long. The final pope will be a tool of the Antichrist. The Roman church is already a tool of the Antichrist, indirectly supporting his aims, even though they may not be aware of it.

(Centurie II, Quatrain 57)

The last three popes of the Catholic Church will fall in short succession. The third to the last will die from an assassin's shooting. The second-to-last will be "swallowed up" by the schemings of the Antichrist. The last, the one born slightly misshapen, will go the greatest distance in destroying the church. The Antichrist will use him for awhile until he gets in the way, at which point he is eliminated. His treachery will accelerate, and his death will signal, the end of the Catholic Church.

2.5. Assassination of the current pope

(Centurie VIII, Quatrain 46)

During the period that the Antichrist begins to flex his power, the current pope will be assassinated when he goes on a trip away from the Vatican. The two cardinals nearest to the pope will realize the danger to their church after the death, and they will close themselves up in the Vatican to try to protect themselves.

The current Pope is desirous of world peace and is working against some established power parties within the Roman church. A point will come when the special interests inside the church who want to hold onto their power and wealth will misadvise the Pope in such a way as to place him in a dangerous situation which he is unaware of. The assassination will lead to social unrest and rioting in Rome. The next pope will not last long. There will be only two other popes after the present one.

(Centurie II, Quatrain 97)

The pope and several of his entourage will be assassinated in late spring when the roses bloom, at a European city that is at the junction of two major rivers.

(Centurie II, Quatrain 15)

The present pope will be assassinated shortly prior to the appearance of a comet that will be clearly visible from the sky of the Northern Hemisphere. His concern for the human condition, leading him to treacherous travel arrangements, wil be his downfall. The next pope will be assassinated by the Antichrist because he won't submit to his demands. The assassination allows the Antichrist to install his "tool" into the office.

2.6. Second-to-last pope "swallowed" by Antichrist's scheming

(Centurie I, Quatrain 4)

The second-to-last pope instated after the assassination of the current one will have a short reign. Due to political blunders and mistakes he will pave the way for the final pope to be a tool of the Antichrist. His reign is an omen of the final downfall of the church.

(Centurie II, Quatrain 36)

Before the Antichrist comes to full power it will appear that other leaders are above him and in control of the power structure other than him. In reality the Antichrist is using them as stepping stones in his quest for world power. During this period he will have traitorous cardinal working for him, spying on the second-to-last pope. One of the cardinals will steal information from him and alter the pope's personal correspondence, so that it has different connotations. It will make the situation appear inordinately worse than it is in reality, causing the pope to react inappropriately. This way the populace will be more likely to see him as incompetent and destabilize his authority, possibly by being assassinated. The cardinal will be troubled by his betrayal because of the obvious dissension it causes the Church, but he is allied with the Antichrist and will rationalize away his backstabbing.

2.7. The treachery of the final pope

(Centurie III, Quatrain 65)

The last pope will be elected shortly after the discovery of the tomb of an ancient Roman whose philosophies greatly influence western thought, something like within a year's time. This is the "poisonous" pope that is actually only a tool for the Antichrist who will bring about the ultimate destruction of the Catholic Church.

The last pope will probably be French, with a swarthy complexion and blue eyes. There will be an air of mystery to him. He will have a physical deformity of some sort, like a slightly hunched shoulder or clubfoot, a congenital defect in the bone (It won't be caused by injury, he was born with it.) His mind has been scarred by the deformity and the cruelty and callousness of people toward others who are different.

He entered the church at a young age out of bitterness and desperation because he knew he would never get a girl to love and marry him. His parents were involved with the Nazi movement in France and his schoolmates taunted him with names like "Nazi lover". This pope could have been kindly if it weren't for his childhood environment and experiences, but instead was warped into cruelty from pain, and he wants to "get back" at the world for his suffering while young. This is a weakness that the Antichrist exploits.

This pope will want to show his enemies, "look at me; I'm powerful; I can do it; I'm better than you." After he attains the power he desires, he will be indirectly responsible for the murder of innocent people because of his alignment with the Antichrist. He will not murder anyone himself, but will open up avenues for the Antichrist to do so, particularly those who hurt him when he was young. This future pope now appears to be kindly on the surface because it is advantageous for him to be perceived that way, but the sinister side of his personality is deeply rooted.

(Centurie II, Quatrain 76)

The final pope will betray his Church by revealing extremely crucial and sensitive information directly to the Antichrist,

16

information that the Antichrist could never have obtained even through his spies in the church.

2.8. Demise of the Catholic Church

(Centurie X, Quatrain 70)

Ruin will befall the Catholic Church because of its leaders' ambition for illegitimate power. The leaders will become vainglorious and think that they can handle whatever they desire to grasp, and it will be their downfall. Their ambitions will be chilled when they fail and the church will be subject to great upheaval, with the Pope ultimately being dethroned. Catholics will become disillusioned with the power mongering, will no longer support the church, and the sphere of influence of the Church will greatly diminish.

(Centurie V, Quatrain 25)

The base of the Catholic Church in Rome will be destroyed in an accident, as if the city sank into the sea. This will somewhat coincide with events in the Middle east and some people will connect the two, but in reality it is a coincidence. However the Arabs will quickly take advantage of the situation even though they didn't cause it. The restrictions of the Vatican will cause the church to crumble. They may rally, but it will be a blow they will never recover from.

The downfall will reveal why the church finally collapsed after surviving so many centuries. The accident will be a combination of natural and human-triggered disasters. The force will involve the sea and a great energy force from the sky descending and dissolving the landscape. It will be termed a natural disaster because it's beyond the capability of anyone on the earth to produce the force. No one can find any cause so it is labeled an

"Act of Nature". However, the more important event of the time, which people will be distracted from noticing, is the Antichrist's invasion of Turkey.

2.9. Cabal's teeth in the international power flow

(Centurie II, Quatrain 58)

During the time of the Antichrist a secretive, conspiratorial cabal are "pulling the strings" behind the scenes to manipulate world politics and economies for personal gain. These master puppeteers operate figureheads in many countries, governments, and the major world capitals. They are united but are very clever in disguising their influence. They hold positions that appear to be relatively minor, like advisors and under-secretaries and such, but are key positions of their power.

In the daytime they appear to be good, loyal, model citizens working for the same goals their governments are supposedly working for, but behind the scenes they band together and pool their information and contacts to work for their own ends. They do not appear to have any political power but they really have a firm grip on world affairs, like sharp teeth sunk into everything.

This secret organization has been in existence for several generations. Their existence is hinted in the family histories of the banking powers and money centers of the world. Only the families involved are aware. The cabal of leaders has been very slowly but surely building up a worldwide network of power, because they want to take over but stay behind the scenes.

At first when the Antichrist comes along the leaders of the Cabal regard him as a new, dynamic, youthful leader from the Middle

East they can use to unite the area and reign it into their realm of control. But the Antichrist ends up turning the tables on them.

2.10. Cabal involved in military and economic conquests

(Centurie II, Quatrain 88)

The Antichrist successfully takes over nearly all of Europe. The cabal of international financiers and bankers will not stay in active war with the Antichrist and his attention will turn elsewhere. In France the underground will begin to flourish.

The Cabal families made their influence and fortunes in the banking and commodities industries, such as gold or diamond mines, leather, tins, etc, like the colonial barons associated with the European world empires who started their families' fortunes exploiting the materials of the Third World nations. "The seventh and the fifth" will have the same names, and the seventh one will be considered part of the fifth.

The Cabal manipulates the economy to cause the unemployment or inflation rates to rise or fall at their whim. They have affected everyone's life.

2.10. Cabal destroyed by the Antichrist

(Centurie II, Quatrain 18)

Somehow through the espionage powers of the Antichrist, the seven key leaders of the secret cabal will be discovered and destroyed. This is his familiar technique of throwing his enemies into confusion and chaos to seize or take advantage of their assets in their weakened state. At the time he knew only that they were financing the European forces that opposed him.

But in this case it is shortsighted of him because it was the cabal that has been instigating the warfare going on through the decades and centuries, and destroying them in effect seals the "beginning of the end" for the Antichrist because their hidden activities promoted his agenda. When they are removed the agitation for world war is no longer present and the natural inclination for world peace will assert itself, thereby doing away with the Antichrist.

2.11. Fundamentalist fanatics' infiltrations into governments

(Centurie I-40)

Powerful men involved with fundamentalist religion and politics, shrewd in manipulation, propaganda, and in distorting the word of God for their own ends will band together to obtain *key* posts in the government. The posts are not necessarily splashy or public but are critical points in the power flow where they can exert their influence to subtly affect world events in their favor.

Leaders in the Middle East will become aware and alarmed by their encroachments and will change their laws, making it more difficult for Americans to travel in this area. It will affect American money, currencies, and trade with the U.S. The Antichrist, in the midst of building a power base, will be influenced by these actions, in a way that will be harmful to the Christian cause later. The religious fundamentalists will cause their own undoing in this way.

2.12. Manipulation of the IRA in Ireland by the underworld

(Centurie VI, Quatrain 62)

Members of the underworld will send faulty arms and drugs to fighters in Ireland. The British and the IRA both believe they are fighting for the good of the country but at the last minute realize they have been destroying it. At the last minute they will try to compromise but will be foiled by the manipulations of the underworld conspirators who are playing each side against the other. The underworld elements are spread in many areas but the arms and drugs will be shipped from Monaco.

2.13. Wealthy U.S. businessman a closet revolutionary and Nazi

(Centurie V, Quatrain 75)

A very wealthy and famous businessman in the U.S. will be secretly involved with the American Nazi Party and the Ku Klux Klan in the south. The man's sole ambition in life is to overthrow the American government as it is presently constituted. The man will be involved with politics but will stay low-key, spinning webs of power and expanding his influence behind the scenes. This groundwork will prove useful for the Antichrist later on. The man will have a puppet, a figurehead, but he will pull the strings. The link will not be known until the time of the Antichrist.

2.14. Fundamentalist censorship

(Centurie II, Quatrain 85)

A distortion in religious values will plague the populace during the times of troubles. Fundamentalist religion and its fanatics will be like an old man holding a thick oaken stick over his followers, to make sure they don't step out of line. This is opposed to spirit of honor, valor, loyalty to one's country, and all the other virtues. The fundamentalists will be both Christian and Moslem.

(Centurie I, Quatrain 62)

During the time of troubles and massive earth upheavals, the countries that harbor fundamentalist religions and philosophies will become very powerful, claiming to offer the true comfort and path for the populace in need. The fundamentalist groups will suppress learning and education and censor books.

2.15. Terrorist assassinations

(Centurie IX, Quatrain 36)

The final pope is captured into the influence of the Antichrist during a period of great civil unrest, war, and desolation, and many other horrible events. History will be seen as a series of catastrophic events, each topping the ones before, leading up to the time of troubles.

During the time of troubles the assassination of world leaders will become extremely common, so much that the population will not even keep track of who is the current leader, thinking it a futile exercise because they are assassinated so frequently. With the warfare going on, a great danger will exist to anyone who has ambitions for leadership, except for the Antichrist, who will be actually orchestrating most of the assassinations himself.

Part III: The Antichrist

3.1. Antichrist's rise to power in Middle East

(Centurie III, Quatrain 34)

The Antichrist will spend many years working silently behind the scenes to consolidate his power, and make his appearance onto the international arena once the structure is in place. He will have planned carefully and the countries he goes against will be unprepared for his golden-tongued treachery.

(Centurie VIII, Quatrain 77)

The Antichrist is the power behind the scenes, pulling the strings, and has not yet made his move to reveal himself. He is like a spider waiting for his time, taking advantage of the world situation to make his move.

When his time comes he will take advantage of the political situation in a country to rise to power. It will not matter that he is not a native of the country. He will take advantage of loopholes and contrive positions. He may aggressively and audaciously seize a position in a military organization after his uncle dies, for example.

23

(Centurie I, Quatrain 34)

The Antichrist will foment rebellions within the countries he's aiming to take over. He will allow the various political splinter groups to believe he supports their cause, when he is actually playing them against each other. The countries will turn in on themselves, weakening them for his outside conquest.

(Centurie II, Quatrain 23)

The Antichrist will take over Iran by using a human decoy to trick the Ayatollah in power. This will involve the "yes men" and sycophants of the Ayatollah's court. The Antichrist will first drive away internal supporters of the Ayatollah by starting a civil war. Then he will put forth a man as a leader, a man for Iranians loyal to the Ayatollah to concentrate their hate on. The man will be assassinated while Iran is being taken over, and his opponents will think they have foiled the overthrow of power by assassinating him. But they will find out later he was merely a decoy and that they played into the plans of the Antichrist.

(Centurie II, Quatrain 81)

The Antichrist will initially obtain power in his own sphere, Asia, and the Middle East. As he grows out of this arena, i.e. into Europe, the next step will be into the Mediterranean, approaching from the south, his area of strength. Because of his Middle Eastern heritage he will have already united North Africans, who are sympathetic to his cultural background, with his Asian and Middle Eastern conglomerate.

3.2. Antichrists' unified monetary system

(Centurie I, Quatrain 40)

The Antichrist will start uniting the monetary systems of his region to help merge them into a single political entity. His ambition to rule the world will be advanced by instituting a single currency with others going defunct. There will be a resistance to this, particularly by a popular, charismatic leader from Egypt, demanding the edict and law be withdrawn that requires the Arab nations give up their currencies and be submissive to the unified political conglomerate.

3.3. Antichrist's seizure of Asia

(Centurie IV, Quatrain 50)

The Antichrist will take over Asia by appointing sub commanders to rule vast tracts of land for him. But their ties to him will be masked and the world will not realize they are merely puppets until a succession of them are installed in the place of predecessors. At first the U.S. will not interfere because it is thought the government was freely chosen by the people, but only later realize the leaders were forced on the populace as mouthpieces and tools for the Antichrist.

(Centurie III, Quatrain 95)

Russia will be his first major Asian conquest and he will do it not through force but through guile and his compelling persuasiveness. He will trick the Russians to come under his power and there will be nothing they can do about it. They will think they are acting in their own best interests. The Middle East will be mostly under his control before he turns to Russia. Then he turns to China and the rest of the Asian continent, to build a position to take over the entire world. He will not trick the Chinese but will some other method.

3.4. Antichrist's cultural eradication & European campaign

(Centurie II, Quatrain 15)

When the second pope is assassinated, the Antichrist will begin his European campaign. The Prime Minister of Britain and the U.S. President will go into consultation over the matter. They will meet at sea like Churchill and Roosevelt did for better security and secrecy of the meetings.

(Centurie II, Quatrain 81)

During the use of his weapons and the ravages of war, one of the devastatingly effective plans of attack by the Antichrist is to threaten the destruction of the victim's cultural centers, not so much physical destruction of the populace. Because the population attributes great value to places and artifacts with large historical and cultural significance, the terrorist-extortionist technique will be very powerful in striking fear into his foe and "bringing them to their knees".

To put Europe into an initial shock, he will begin to smash and destroy the city of Rome to rubble via aerial bombing raids. It will be destroyed to such an extent that the "seven hills of Rome" will be leveled. Rome will be so annihilated as to be threatened by an encroachment from the sea, destroying all that is left.

He will also threaten the cultural centers of Greece and the great Greek cultural centers of learning, including Athens. Most cultural treasures and major metropolitan centers of the entire peninsula will be destroyed. The world leaders will be momentarily shocked and paralyzed by his barbarity. In the presence of their indecisiveness and absence of their action he will make great strides in taking over territory and governments. The Antichrist will continually use shocking and unprecedented moves like these to advance his domination throughout the entire WWWIII.

The eradication of cultural treasures also fits in with the Antichrist's ulterior motive of wiping out the established culture to supplant it with his own, like the Moors attempted when they invaded Spain, except in his case on the level of an entire continent.

(Centurie II, Quatrain 84)

Drought and weather changes will take place during the time of troubles. The Antichrist will take over Italy and Greece by destroying the cultural centers to devastate morale of the subjugated citizens.

3.5. Antichrist's ravage of the Catholic Church

(Centurie V, Quatrain 43)

In addition to the cultural destruction of European cultural centers, the Antichrist will ransack the Vatican library with the intent of ultimately destroying it. He will do this to undermine the authority of the Vatican and break up the power fragments that remain. One way he will do this is by revealing important, controversial material hidden in the Vatican library that the Catholic Church will be seen to have suppressed because of the threat to its authority. This will cause major schisms in the church as priests and students turn against each other in their theories and interpretations of the new material. The confusion and chaos will remove the Catholic Church as an obstacle to the Antichrist's plans.

(Centurie I, Quatrain 62)

The ransacking of the Vatican library by the Antichrist will bring to light and open to the world information, facts, and knowledge that had been suppressed for several centuries. Even though he uses violence, the Antichrist will actually be burning off his karma because of the positive effects of the release, starting a new cycle, higher cycle of his karma.

(Centurie II, Quatrain 12)

The people involved with the Catholic church, particularly the priests, will cling to the old order even though it is not viable and dead as far as working within the reality of the changed times. The Antichrist and the last pope will be "robbing blind" the Church. The Antichrist will desecrate and raid the Vatican library and cart away the treasures of the church to help fund his armies. The Catholic Church will become totally superfluous, and contribute to its own demise.

3.6. Antichrist's invasion of Turkey

(Centurie V, Quatrain 25)

When the Catholic Church in Rome is finally destroyed in a devastating but mysterious "Act of Nature", people will be distracted from noticing the more important event of the time, the Antichrist invading Turkey.

(Centurie II, Quatrain 29,V-54)

After the destruction in Italy wrought by the Antichrist, he will go over the mountains through France via airplane. He will attack Europe from the south because he will have the solid backing of the Islamic world and will already have bloodily subjugated North Africa and the Middle East. He will set up regional headquarters in Turkey, and other outposts, to rule and advance further conquests.

3.7. Switzerland alarmed by Antichrist's Nazism in Germany

(Centurie I, Quatrain 61)

While the Antichrist is in the process of taking over Europe, he will back the Nazi Party in Germany. The current popularity of Nazism among the youth of Germany will lay the groundwork for this. Eventually Switzerland will become alarmed and break its centuries-old tradition of neutrality, taking the side against the Antichrist and actively fighting.

(Centurie II, Quatrain 39)

Infiltrators, spies, and traitors in Germany, France, Spain, and Italy will be secretly working for the Antichrist's cause of taking over Europe. The education establishment will be abandoned because it is unsupportable during wartime.

3.8. International (non) reaction to the Antichrist

(Centurie II, Quatrain 96)

Diplomatic foul-ups in other countries will permit the Antichrist to attain greater power. In the beginning, when he does not have a broad base of power but is building on it, those in power elsewhere who can do something about it will hesitate until it is too late. Even though people realize he wields great power "from the dark side", his demonic hatred and magnetism will enhance the fatal attraction. He will advance his campaign by invading and conquering neighboring countries, particularly because of the political turmoil and instability of the realm. Eventually he will subdue the entire Asian continent under his rule. The Antichrist will be in this period of increasing his power during the visit of the comet visible from the Northern hemisphere in about 7.

(Centurie I, Quatrain 37)

The U.S. will vacillate in dissension during the conquests of the Antichrist. Its power, influence, and "can do" capabilities will have diminished in the international arena at the time. The populace will argue over involvement vs. noninvolvement. Shipping will be very dangerous because of submarine warfare practiced by the Antichrist. Enemy soldiers in foreign ports will foul up sea-based commerce. Many decisive battles in his wars will involve seaports. Many people will die far away from home in the war.

(Centurie III, Quatrain 7)

The various weaker countries threatened by the Antichrist's imperialism will call on stronger ones for help, like the U.S. which will initially be neutral and uncommitted. The Antichrist will be attempting to take over part of the world using aerial warfare. In one battle in the night a squadron of unmarked planes will rebuff his advance, sent secretly by the U.S.

(Centurie V, Quatrain 86)

Responsive, proactive countermeasures could have prevented the destruction caused by the Antichrist but the political and diplomatic strife among the Western powers will have failed to have "nipped the situation in the bud". England and the U.S. will have enough military power to confront the Antichrist but because of lack of consensus neither will act quickly. A newly established alliance between the two is only in its infancy at the time, and the powers have not established the authority of overall decision-making in time. Also, a breakdown in communications and transportation will cause important political analysts to be cut off from advising the leaders. Meanwhile the Antichrist will be making conquests in leaps and bounds.

Part IV: The Time of Troubles

Prelude to the Antichrist and WWWIII

4.1. Volcanoes, earthquakes, floods, droughts, famines, rioting
4.2. Death of world leader and revolt coincides with comet
4.3. Fiasco from communication breakdown between two superpowers
4.4. Russian/American submarine/naval confrontation
4.5. Crazed leader launches atom bombs on Mediterranean and Europe
4.6. Third world country leader creates strife
4.7. Antichrist profits from radar research in Europe

International political and social incidents

4.8. War-game simulation by Britain in Europe leads to disaster
4.9. American Electoral College voting stalemate
4.10. Earth abuse causes agricultural devastation in U.S. and Britain
4.11. Underwater Russian submarine base defanged by diplomacy
4.12. Extraterrestrials shot by paranoid nation, bacteriological agents released
4.13. Extraterrestrial probe of the Watchers discovered by scientists

---

4.1. Volcanoes, earthquakes, floods, droughts, famines, rioting

(Centurie IV, Quatrain 67)

A very bright, previously unknown comet will appear and coincide with the time of great geological troubles, with earthquakes and volcanoes erupting and disrupting weather systems. This will cause widespread famines and droughts, and social upheavals in unexpected places. Nations that are considered prosperous and powerful, particularly western nations will be weakened. They will be torn with civil strife and rioting as people migrate to areas that have water and can support crop-growing. The social upheaval and weakening of political structures will help the Antichrist come to power.

(Centurie VIII, Quatrain 29)

A great and rich power will be subject to serious natural disasters, particularly earthquakes and flooding, and rend the nation from end to end, causing enormous conflict, despair, and misery. The wealthy power will be bankrupted attempting to deal with its disasters. Three other great nations will send aid to help the citizens survive.

Earth changes will take place that will help the Antichrist's drive for world conquest. In central Europe, southern Europe, and in the Near East, particularly around the eastern end of the Mediterranean, there'll be severe floods. As a result of the disruption to local governments by the natural disasters, the Antichrist will move his troops in under the disguise of helping the people restore civil order, but really use this as a device to take over countries, and to use the populations like slaves.

Serious economic problems will persist along with great social unrest, contributing to the ease with which the Antichrist can seize power. The frightened and hopeful populace will be vulnerable to his demagoguery. The Antichrist will use the disasters as opportunities to overthrow governments and sneak spies into a country. Martial law will be declared in many areas to stop rioting and looting. The Middle East, the source of his power, will not be as devastated as the rest of the world. He

33

offers assistance to other countries trying to recover but he will eventually stab them in the back.

4.2. Death of world leader and revolt coincides with comet

(Centurie II, Quatrain 62)

The death of a world leader will coincide with the appearance of a comet. The comet will be clearly visible where the leader dies. The country is in the Middle East. The death of the leader and widespread crop failures and hunger in that year will provoke a revolt. It will start when the comet is visible but will continue for five hundred days. Also, a hundred people will contribute to the revolt in such a way that it will break forth and become open enough and wide-spread enough to capture the world's attention.

4.3. Fiasco from communication breakdown between two superpowers

(Centurie II, Quatrain 48)

Through a mistake by a leader an international incident will occur. The main problem will be a breakdown in communications between the two powers involved. The situation is a lot more complex than will appear on the surface. The chief, the leader involved, will feel great regret about what happened and will want to continue his career and help correct the situation, to help make up for the adverse affects of it.

But he will be hung, symbolically, by others wishing to take his position in the organization. He will be hung so far as politics and his career are concerned. It will almost be like committing suicide because in the end he will be a broken man and not be able to do anything about the situation. The entire event will be viewed as a fiasco from both sides. It will have very harmful and even cataclysmic consequences.

The situation develops when an enemy or one who is against the U.S. will take advantage of the incident in an unethical way, by sending a horde of agents working for their side into this area. The world will be outraged by the action.

(Centurie II, Quatrain 35)

A breakdown in communications between the US and Russia will result in a misunderstanding and deep resentments between the Kremlin and the White House. Some will risk their careers to try to tame the situation but will be silenced, and "burned" such as by demotions to obscure positions.

4.4. Russian/American submarine/naval confrontation

(Centurie II, Quatrain 48)

In the southwest quadrant of the Atlantic Ocean, missiles will splash into the ocean near a partially submerged ship and a submarine. The submarine commander is antsy to engage fire. An American surface ship will be in danger. The Russian commander of the sub will have secret orders the rest of the crew is not aware of, which are to antagonize and provoke. He gets carried away.

The American commander has been ordered to defend the coast of the US but to avoid starting a war. In the process of defending his ship from the submarine, he strikes the submarine and feels he may have sunk it, and agonizes that the action would be interpreted as starting a war and not an act of defense. The event will lead to the time of troubles and will have large historical significance when seen in retrospect.

4.5. Crazed leader launches atom bombs on Mediterranean and Europe

(Centurie II, Quatrain 3)

During continuing unrest in the Middle East, one of the leaders will be able to get a hold of an atom bomb. He will be crazy and go to the greatest lengths over the smallest thing and will not hesitate to use the weapon because his obsessions with deadly warfare. The people he is warring against retaliate with a nuclear weapon. The country has a coast on the Mediterranean.

One of the bombs will land in the Mediterranean instead of the land, poisoning all the fish. The passages of trade in the region will be disrupted so that the people on the other coast of the Mediterranean will be desperate for food and will eat the fish anyway. It will happen near the east coast of the Mediterranean in a region of dark-colored cliffs.

(Centurie II, Quatrain 4)

The atomic weapon being dropped by one of the Middle Eastern countries will spark off yet another war on top of that war. European and Western nations will try to interfere to diminish the threat to oil supplies. When the European countries try to interfere, the crazed leader who earlier dropped the atomic bomb will use the rest of his arsenal on Europe, most striking the closer southern part.

The European Mediterranean coast, particularly that of Italy and France, will be almost uninhabitable, and Italy will get the brunt. This leader is not the Antichrist but helps to set the stage for the

36

Antichrist to rise to power with little or no opposition. The Antichrist will wield great power and authority; no one can argue with him.

4.6. Third world country leader creates strife

(Centurie III, Quatrain 60)

A "young dark man" will arise as a leader in a Third World country; his main goal is to unite the other Third World countries to do battle with the superpowers. The area of conflict will be in Eastern Europe and the Middle East, particularly around the Adriatic and the Caspian seas and the eastern Mediterranean. No definite winner will emerge but the strife will help set the stage for the Antichrist. Some prophecies in the Bible refer to events in this region (Israel will be involved).

4.7. Antichrist profits from radar research in Europe

(Centurie I, Quatrain 6)

Research on a more sophisticated type of radar and sensing devices will give greater information to the operator, i.e. an airplane pilot. But the first experiments with the technology will fail in a disastrous accident, when the "sympathetic vibrations" emitted by the device cause the chassis of the plane to become weakened and dangerous due to dissolved bonds of the molecules in the metal. The scientists involved with the research will have to temporarily abandon the research because of diplomatic breakdowns, the threat of war, etc.

This will take place before the Antichrist comes to full power. It will happen in Europe at the time the Antichrist is strengthening his base of power in the Middle East. The devices are currently under development but have not been tested yet. But this is another historical event that will permit the Antichrist to take over Europe.

4.8. War game simulation by Britain in Europe leads to disaster

(Centurie II, Quatrain 2)

In a war-game maneuver involving Great Britain and European troops a malfunctioning circuit in a computer will cause the "real-world" situation to play out instead of the simulation. The teams are labeled "white" and "blue". As a result of the error actual defenses will be activated and real bombs will be dropped on the areas of the game and cause a tragic international incident.

4.9. American Electoral College voting stalemate

(Centurie VII, Quatrain 41)

The presidents of the U.S., a supposedly free country, have been abusing their power to an increasingly greater extent. During a time of social unrest even more so than the period of Viet Nam and Watergate, the Electoral College will be evenly split over the election of the new president. The process will stalemate, with many people clamoring for whichever candidate they voted for, causing enormous tension in the country. Internationally it will be a sensitive situation.

Because of the split, and the extremely volatile and explosive social unrest, putting either candidate in office instead of the other could start a civil war or a revolution. After a long time of impassioned speeches invoking patriotism and the founding fathers, a compromise solution of holding another election will be taken, and a candidate will be installed without disaster.

4.10. Earth abuse causes agricultural devastation in U.S. and Britain

(Centurie II, Quatrain 95)

Man will upset the balance of the earth and cause great changes in the climate and seasons, causing much hardship and famine. Major agricultural lands producing a lot of grain and food for the world today will become frozen and will be unusable. The people who live on this land and grow the food will flee like rats leaving a sinking ship.

There will be dissension and fighting over the land. As a result of the panic, incompetent decisions are made by the people in power under enormous stress. Poor decisions will escalate into major disasters. The U.S. and the United Kingdom in particular will experience the dissension and destruction.

4.11. Underwater Russian submarine base defanged by diplomacy

(Centurie III, Quatrain 21)

The Russians have built an experimental underwater submarine base and dome in the Adriatic sea. They use it for subversive submarine operations. When it is discovered, due to pressure from statesmen, diplomats, and politicians, it will be brought to the surface and the submarines will be taken away through political maneuverings.

4.12. Extraterrestrials shot by paranoid nation, bacteriological agents released

(Centurie II, Quatrain 91)

Extraterrestrials tried to contact us in the Siberia Tunguska explosion in the 0s. Similarly they will again visit the earth. The Russians are doing secret weapons research and have energy fields guarding northern approach corridors. Another spacecraft will arrive, paralleling this incident. When the extraterrestrial spacecraft enters the atmosphere the fields will cause it to malfunction and many of the crew are killed.

When they crash, soldiers will be on hand to capture or kill them. The ship will harbor microorganisms that will react in bizarre ways to the earth climate and cause plagues of unknown origin, which cannot be understood because of the extraterrestrial causative organism. The country will be at war or fixing to go to war and will have a paranoid mindset. Thinking the crash is a result of enemy weapons, the soldiers will shoot anything that moves.

4.13. Extraterrestrial probe of the Watchers discovered by scientists

(Centurie IV, Quatrain 28)

During the time of troubles, when the sun is between the earth and Venus, i.e. from the point of view of Earth Venus is hidden by the sun, the Watchers (extraterrestrials) will be exposed through the powers of observation and communication. Scientists involved with radiotelescopy and related disciplines will observe an anomaly, and as they focus on it they come to the realization

40

that it is a strong indication of a real UFO. The readings are caused by an instrument sent by the Watchers to observe mankind.

The scientists and the populace will learn more about the probe and the Watchers. But internal dissension will be created by fundamentalists because the existence of extraterrestrials is not consistent with their worldview. This will take place in approximately 7 or 8. The Watchers are returning to mankind at this time because they are trying to help him through gentle prodding and increasing spiritual love. They have always kept an eye on us and have observed our growth and development. They're looking forward to the day we can join the universal community and help with their project in a way that's unique to us.

Part V: Scientific Achievements in the Time of Troubles

Technology accidents

5.1. Nostradamus on the dangers of weaponry mixed with natural disaster
5.2. Weather modulation devices go awry, cause ice and hail
5.3. Nuclear reactor meltdown near city with underground chambers
5.4. Space shuttle accident releases microorganisms into atmosphere
5.5. Devastating accidental weaponry explosions from earth tumult
5.6. Ruptured earth energy fields cause meteorite storm
5.7. Research into warping time leads to disaster

The weapons of WWWIII

5.8. New, horrific, secret, radical weapons monstrosities in WWW III
5.9. The top-secret earthquake-triggering weapon (ETW)
5.10. ETW unleashed on San Andreas and New Madrid Faults
5.11. Atomic device creates greenhouse effect, devastates agriculture
5.12. Death by the "milky rain" weapon
5.13. "Explosion of light" causes horrible birth defects
5.14. Diplomacy dies with international earthquake terrorism
5.15. Death by radio waves

Eugenics

5.16. Human eugenics research advanced by the King of Terror
5.17. Eugenics scientists meet grisly deaths from public backlash

5.1. Nostradamus on the dangers of weaponry mixed with natural disaster

To avoid the worst effects of the pole shift, "Stop the explosions that the military feels are so important." Understand that what happens with your weaponry will have a large effect on how much or how soon this devastation [of the shift] would occur. Make people aware of the damage that can occur to their present weaponry system. IF people become more aware of the damage that can be caused by the military destruction, whether voluntary or involuntary-- if this can be prevented, the reaction set off beneath the earth's surface would be less damaging It is the earth changes that will be causing the danger of the weaponry, not the use of it. Accidents will occur in the New World, because of natural earthquakes. The results that would happen from an earthquake near one of your military housing of the weaponry would cause your leaders to definitely realize the dangers

5.2. Weather modulation devices go awry, cause ice and hail

(Centurie I, Quatrain 22)

Devices developed by man to manipulate the weather will go awry because of faulty programming. They will cause a great deal of damage through unseasonal ice and hail. The scientists don't understand the forces they are dealing with and that the natural weather pattern will overcome interference in attempting to attain proper balance. The computers will fight the increasing intensity and break, damaged beyond use.

5.3. Nuclear reactor meltdown near city with underground chambers

(Centurie X, Quatrain 49)

In the US, in the Rocky Mountains, a complete city will be built near to underground chambers blasted into a mountain for the storage of secret records. The water pumped into a nuclear reactor will not be totally purified, and an element in the reactor will cause a meltdown, unleashing radioactive poison.

5.4. Space shuttle accident releases microorganisms into atmosphere

(Centurie II, Quatrain 65)

Incompetent leaders, who got their position by family prestige, in a joint space venture between America and France, will be behind an accident involving a space shuttle. The ship will have scientists on board doing biological experiments to see the effect out of the reach of gravity. An accident and malfunction will cause the ship to lose orbit, break up and burn on reentry. Some of the microorganisms on board survive the fall. They will have the potential of causing plagues.

5.5. Devastating accidental weaponry explosions from earth tumult

With the earthquakes and volcanoes will be accidental explosion of the weaponry that is buried in the ground. This is going to cause great emotional turmoil within the U.S. and [Britain and France].

44

The countries in Europe will want disarmament. It is important they realize that if this disarmament of the weapons comes about, that will take place in the Moslem countries also.

5.6. Ruptured earth energy fields cause meteorite storm

(Centurie I, Quatrain 46)

Research scientists will be investigating the powers associated with the various energy fields of the earth. They'll try to harness the powers for different purposes, including warfare. When they begin experiments, in an area near the North Sea they will accidentally rupture one of the earth's fields so that a beam of energy will shoot out into space and draw a steady stream of meteorites to earth. They will continue to rain down until the scientists can repair the damage. Doing so will cause an earthquake from built-up stress. The research will be a secret government project. To the world at large this will appear to be a natural phenomenon and will be recorded as such in future history books, because the government will keep the project concealed even after the accident.

5.7. Research into warping time leads to disaster

(Centurie III, Quatrain 92)

Scientists are researching how to warp and alter time to help change the outcome of a war. Near the end of a war, after the second failure, the research complex is destroyed in a large catastrophe. Because they are dealing with powers they don't know how to control it rips them apart. People not there assume they were hit by a missile of some sort because of the destruction.

But what really happened was that the vortexes of energy they were trying to deal with were not fine tuned enough to work with and they got out of control. It appears to involve England and Northern Europe. It's in our future but the groundwork has been laid already by scientists working on secret projects in this direction. Something may come of it in our lifetimes but the government will keep it under wraps.

The catastrophe will be very localized and will have some strange side-effects in the dimension of time in the general area there. The government was counting on it to give it an edge in the war and loses it and will end up affecting the outcome of the war.

5.8. New, horrific, secret, radical weapons monstrosities in WWWIII

(Centurie IV, Quatrain 33)

Advanced technology that is currently being developed in secret, referred to in other quatrains, will play a part in the time of troubles. This will coincide with great famine, plagues, and destruction with the onset of WWWIII.

Nations will be desperate and will try anything to stop the Antichrist. Scientists will search for new, even more radical weapons for warfare that almost defy belief.

(Centurie II, Quatrain 32)

Instruments of death built and refined during the time of the Antichrist will wreak great destruction. Variations on atomic weaponry and other devices will be developed. The ultimate monstrosity in weapons will be created near Ravenna, culminating research that is currently in progress during the time of troubles. The weapons will particularly disrupt the natural earth ecology. All sides in WWWIII will "have their fair share" of horrible weapons.

(Centurie IV, Quatrain 30)

The space program will fall into disfavor through policy changes in the government with the emphasis shifted in a different direction than space exploration. The change is due to some nefarious policy making behind the scenes the voting public is not aware of but would not approve of if they knew about it. The policy changes of redirecting the money toward military applications will contribute to the horrors of the changes that are to come. The machinations behind the scenes will not be exposed until a later date.

5.9. The top-secret earthquake-triggering weapon (ETW)

(Centurie IX, Quatrain 83)

A weapon will developed in secret underground laboratories that can trigger earthquakes at existing fault zones. It will work from a scientific principle recently discovered but not yet developed. The weapon will involve an airplane or airborne origination that may drop something or project a laser ray onto a region. An extension of the device is carried in a plane that flies over the area and focuses energy waves where the earthquake is to be triggered. The more technologically complex power source will be based and channeled from the secret laboratory via the plane.

The country that develops this will be able to hold it as a major threat against major nations, because most nations have geological faults that are susceptible to earthquakes and therefore the weapon. The situation will parallel the development of the atomic bomb by the U.S. in that the country will be the sole owner and the capability for destruction will be so awe-inspiring and frightening that everyone, including the infidels, will call upon the saints for protection.

During the time of radical earth changes this weapon will be applied to create many earthquakes, generally before the Antichrist comes to power. The nation that develops the machine builds it independent of the Antichrist's forces, but later when he gains greater power he will be able to acquire the weapon. He'll seize the machine for his own agenda of worldwide conquest. The Antichrist will acquire the machine through deceit, trickery, spies, bribery, and all other nefarious means known to man.

5.10. ETW unleashed on San Andreas and New Madrid Faults

The weapon will not be revealed immediately to the world. Only after the country actually uses it and there is an earthquake generated by it, followed by many others that occur without the characteristic buildup of geological pressure, will people become suspicious. The initial earthquake triggered by the weapon will be sufficient to cause other earthquakes in a chain reaction. The San Andreas and New Madrid faults in the U.S. will be affected. The San Andreas will continually rumble and vibrate as a result of the earthquakes triggered by the weapon, in time driving the New Madrid fault to eventually erupt explosively and violently. Initially geologists will think the earthquakes are due to natural causes but later information will point elsewhere and they'll begin to be suspicious. After more earthquakes and further evidence they will finally confront the scientific world with the mounting evidence that they are not natural.

5.11. Atomic device creates greenhouse effect, devastates agriculture

(Centurie X, Quatrain 70)

A type of atomic device, not exactly a bomb, will be created that when set off can disrupt the planetary climate. It will displace an air mass that will upset the balance of hot and cold, so that a greenhouse effect will get out of balance and run to the extreme, causing drastic changes in the climate, and wreak havoc on agricultural production.

(Centurie X, Quatrain 71)

The earth and the air will freeze as another effect of the atomic device described above. Many countermeasures to the devastating climactic affects will be pursued but they will not succeed, in spite of government announcements urging the population to be calm and not to panic.

A famine is caused by weaponry explosions. Accidents that will affect the crops.

5.12. Death by the "milky rain" weapon

(Centurie II, Quatrain 18)

A "rain of milk" alludes to nuclear weapons with bizarre effects on the weather, including a so-called "radiation rain". The weapons will represent a combination of the worse aspects of nuclear and laser weaponry. The laser weaponry, when it is shot down upon people, will resemble a white substance coming down.

5.13. "Explosion of light" causes horrible birth defects

(Centurie I, Quatrain 64)

In WWWIII some of the weapons will scream through the skies before they hit, terrifying and deadly to the population. An atomic or laser weapon detonated at night will cause victims to think they have seen the sun at night. The weapon produces a huge explosion of light. In addition to vast climactic damage the weapon will produce monstrous birth defects in babies, so that children will look almost "swinish" (i.e. like pigs). Scientists will frantically search for ways to alter the effects of the weapon's effect on newborns. A breakthrough will eventually be made, based on an unexpected source in the animal kingdom.

5.14. Diplomacy dies with international earthquake terrorism

The revelation of the weapon will cause a disintegration of diplomatic nations and the United Nations will eventually dissolve, because the paranoid nation that developed the weapon will not share its technology but instead use it as a method of international terrorism.

5.15 Death by radio waves

(Centurie II, Quatrain 2)

A new type of weapon involving radio waves played at a certain frequency will be developed. At certain frequencies and intensities the energy can cause intense pain in the nerve endings and damage areas of the brain, or even be lethal.

5.16. Human eugenics research advanced by the King of Terror

(Centurie X, Quatrain 72)

In 9 and WWWIII many horrible areas of research will be pursued, including a eugenics project, i.e. breeding humans for selected characteristics. This particular research will have been ongoing for decades. The scientists attempt to bring back some of the less civilized, fiercer humans, still smart but cunning and strong, for the purpose of infantry soldiers. The governments engage the bread humans in battles and the scientists will try to tabulate their performance relative to normal human soldiers.

This will happen during the period of WWWIII and enormous social unrest. U.S., Japan, Russia, and some European countries will be involved. They have the gold to fund the research. A "King of Terror", the "power behind the throne", is in charge of the project. He has enormous secret influence and greatly feared, unchallenged power over policy decisions in various countries.

5.17. Eugenics scientists meet grisly deaths from public backlash

(Centurie I, Quatrain 81)

A secret, isolated panel of scientists will develop super-weapons during the time of troubles. They will somewhat unaware of the worldwide wars because of their seclusion. After the "tide has turned" they are no longer on the winning side and their identities are exposed to the winning side. Their fate will be determined according to their role in participation, with some meeting grisly deaths.

Three scientists in particular with the initials K, Th, and L will meet with particularly dramatic demises. These scientists will be chiefly involved with the eugenics project, one reason the populace's reaction to their endeavors will be so violent. Many scientists are involved but nine head the project. The project was started in the 0s and has been carried on in different countries over the decades since then. It will reach a culmination in the time of troubles.

Part VI: World War III

6.1. Overview: horrible battles, weapons, devastation, death

Because of the new awareness the western civilization has come upon, and because of the accelerated rate of the shifting of the earth's crust, and because of the conjunction of the planets, the war *might* be avoided. Depending on the speed at which the natural events occur. For as in any civilization, when natural disasters occur this is more prominent than military conquest.

(Centurie II, Quatrain 40)

During the time of troubles and WWWIII there will be massive naval, air, and land battles. The ultra-secret weapons that are brought forth will shock and stun the world.

(Centurie VIII, Quatrain 17)

The Antichrist will not hesitate to use bacteriological warfare as well as conventional warfare, causing hunger, fire and plagues. The causative organisms will be more virulent than ever and hence increasingly lethal.

(Centurie II, Quatrain 18)

When the Antichrist is taking over Europe, nuclear weapons will wreak havoc like lighting strikes, and from them a "milky rain" will occur. Weapons currently beyond our imagination will wreak unparalleled devastation. Corpses will litter the landscape. The very earth will "cry out in pain". The Antichrist will be so terrible, horrible, and powerful that the rightful rulers of countries will be utterly terrified and will not do anything to stop his ravages. Entire dynasties will be wiped out.

(Centurie III, Quatrain 19)

Before the Antichrist takes over a place, he will rain down death and destruction so that he can seize without opposition. He will travel far from his resting place in doing this. Some of this devastation will make past heinous events of the prior world wars "look like child's play". Unlike Hitler's "rain of blood" he will use a "rain of blood and milk."

6.2. Nuclear confrontation in the Middle East

(Centurie II, Quatrain 60)

A major nuclear confrontation will occur in the Middle East. The aggressor will have broken a promise not to use nuclear weapons in warfare. Naval fleets kept in the area by other powers will be scattered in ruins from the violence of the blast.

Radioactive fallout and its effect on people, animals, and weather, and erupting volcanoes will turn the water of that part of the ocean a muddy red color. Because of this bodies will appear to float in blood. Because of the blasts and earth changes, rivers will change their course, and political boundary lines based on them will be redrawn.

The U.S. will have a Democratic president at the time. He will get involved with the conflict as a way of trying to stimulate the economy from a depression.

6.3. Mediterranean campaign and the battles of Gibraltar

(Centurie III, Quatrain 10)

The Antichrist, during the Mediterranean campaign, will take over Monaco as a crucial strategic position to advancing to Italy and southern Europe. The successor to Prince Ranier, apparently one of his sons, will be imprisoned after the takeover as an obstacle.

(Centurie I, Quatrain 77)

In the Antichrist's Mediterranean battle Gibraltar will play a key role. The key general, a naval officer, will succeed in saving Gibraltar from the Antichrist's forces but will later die in an automobile accident.

(Centurie I, Quatrain 71)

The Rock of Gibraltar will be a strategic position, captured and retaken three times by various forces.

(Centurie I, Quatrain 98)

Marines on naval battle carriers will confront the Antichrist when he attempts to invade Europe in the area of Crete and Thessaly, but they will be outgunned and have to retreat probably to Gibraltar. In the very fierce and bloody battle the Antichrist will have to transfer many of his troops to a supply ship after a fighting ship is sunk.

6.4. Bomb sent at New York by the Antichrist, France retaliates

(Centurie VI, Quatrain 97)

In WWWIII many existing diplomatic ties between nations will be broken and realigned. One that will continue to hold however is the alliance between France and the U.S. A force aligned with the Antichrist will send a bomb aimed at New York City. It will be spotted and tracked as it approaches. The U.S. defense system will feverishly concentrate on diverting or disabling the bomb, and the U.S. will not be able to retaliate. As proof of their loyalty the French are asked to retaliate, which they do with several bombs and weapons.

The response will be immediate. The American leader uses a hotline to communicate to the French Marshal, who launches self-propelled bombs with "tongues of fire" against the aggressor. In this war some of the bombs will hit New York and some will be diverted. The bomb referred to here will be prematurely detonated along the flight path, saving the city.

Many human lives will be spent when planes flying around the bomb, trying to divert or destroy it, are blown up.

6.5. Bacteriological warfare strikes New York and London

(Centurie II, Quatrain 6)

New York and in London will be hit with scourges from bacteriological warfare, a deadly "bug", either bacteria or virus or some type of disease-causing organism. It will be released into the atmosphere to affect the populations of New York and London. Because of separation and different gene pools, spontaneous mutations in the organisms will affect the two populations in different ways. It will appear to be two different diseases even though it was caused by the same organism.

As a result of this plague the metropolitan infrastructures will break down. The people near but outside the cities will panic and shun the cities and refuse to deliver available food, effectively putting them into quarantine. The city dwellers will starve to death in droves. People will loot and raid stores, and soldiers will stab them off at bayonet point. The government will try to evenly distribute the remaining food but the people will panic and they call on God to relieve them from their misery.

6.6. Antichrist conquers Europe

(Centurie IX, Quatrain 73)

The Antichrist will take over Europe and begin to toy with the idea of establishing some kind of dynasty. Because of his background he is obsessed with power and attracted to the way that a ruling family line can have a major effect on the flow of history, manipulating society over a long span of time through familial line, far beyond the influence of a single individual. But his plans will not materialize because he is overthrown by Ogmios and his monstrosities will be counterbalanced with positive forces to heal the earth, directed by the Great Genius.

6.7. The Antichrist invades Britain

(Centurie II, Quatrain 68)

In his European campaign the Antichrist will attempt to overtake Britain, particularly to seize its naval forces for further advances. England will resist and initially fend off the advance, with support from the U.S. However, it is likely that the Antichrist will eventually overcome England and the more passionate members of the underground will flee to Ireland and Scotland. The Antichrist will not succeed in overtaking the entire island. North England, Scotland, and Ireland will not succumb, possibly aiding the reunification of Ireland to fight the Antichrist. Patriotic and stubborn Irish and Scottish spirit will play a favorable role in turning the tide.

(Centurie III, Quatrain 16)

The British prince, a member of the English royal house, will be eager to lead his troops into battle to defend his own and neighboring countries that have treaties with Britain. He will confront the Antichrist's forces in two major engagements and will be defeated in one. He will be outflanked and will have to retreat in disgrace.

Nevertheless the opposing forces will curse him because he was a valiant fighter, and his brashly engaging in battle disrupted some of the Antichrist's carefully laid plans for the conquest of

58

Europe. The man will return to England and the population will give him a hero's welcome for his bravery despite the defeat.

6.8. The crucial meeting on the naval carrier

(Centurie II, Quatrain 75)

During WWWIII and the great turmoil, an airplane will come for a landing on the deck of an aircraft carrier. It will be from a nation foreign to the country that owns the carrier. The balance of political powers of the two sides involved will be very complex and delicate.

The plane is from a power "slightly more aligned to the other side" although still basically neutral. But to have any kind of contact with the country that owns the carrier would have severe political repercussions relative to the war, so the generals of the carrier are reluctant to give permission to the plane to land. The plane will carry an important political or military leader and an important emissary who needs to deliver important documents and messages. The situation will be very fragile and volatile.

6.9. Seas, rivers, lakes boil; famines lead to insane cannibalism

(Centurie II, Quatrain 75)

During WWWIII shipping and normal trade will be seriously disrupted. Some countries will have excesses of food, such as bushels of wheat, but the price will be so out of proportion that no one will be able to buy it. In countries where there is famine, people will resort to cannibalism to stay alive. The wheat in other countries will be stored in silos and rot because they cannot get rid of it, cannot sell it. The price of the wheat is enormous in cost partly because it is very dangerous to deliver or ship it anywhere during wartime.

(Centurie V, Quatrain 98)

A very great drought will occur in the European continent during the time of the Antichrist. Fish will die as seas, rivers, and lakes boil. The Antichrist will be behind it. This event is not the same but is related to the boiling fish at the Dark Point (, Centurie II, Quatrain 3). Two sites will be in distress from "fire in the sky".

(Centurie II, Quatrain 18)

The extremes in weather during the time of the Antichrist will affect a battle. Extreme rain and hail will take by surprise two armies lined up to do battle. As an alternative plan to confrontation they try to fly planes above the clouds to drop bombs on the opposing forces, "fire and stones falling from the sky".

(Centurie IX, Quatrain 31)

The earth, after a relative period of peace, will suffer a great natural disaster, involving severe earthquakes that rip the crust open, spewing lava. The major earthquake will trigger other earthquakes that will destroy large land areas. Famine and fighting will set in. Countries will fight with each other over surplus food: India and China will march to seize the corn and wheat fields of Russia and eastern Europe. Communications will break down. Religious leaders will lose credibility because of the inability to explain the earth changes. Christianity will falter.

(Centurie I, Quatrain 67)

The climactic changes caused by the detonation of the terrible weapons will cause famines in scattered areas, and conditions will get worse. The uninhabitable regions will continue to grow until the areas connect large surfaces of the earth's land masses, and the majority of humanity will be suffering. People will become virtually insane with the persistent lack of food, and will eat things like tree roots, and even seize newborn infants.

6.10. Antichrist's commander succumbs to key strategic failure

(Centurie VI, Quatrain 33)

The Anti-Christ's supreme commander will make a major failure of judgment on the field in an extremely strategic battle and the bulk of his forces are captured or killed. The supreme commander misuses some technology that has not yet been developed, causing his downfall.

6.11. Russia breaks free of the Antichrist

(Centurie VI, Quatrain 21)

The Antichrist will seem all powerful and all conquering and the situation will appear hopeless. But "his star will be falling" and his power will crack in crucial places. The U.S., Canada, Russia, and later, northern Europe, unite together. In particular, even though the Antichrist has taken over all of Asia, after a period he is no longer able to control Russia. Russia breaks free and unites with the unconquered countries.

The alliance strikes terror into the Antichrist who glimpses the beginning of the end and his potential failure. He chooses another field commander to continue his campaign, but the effort fails. Rhodes and Byzantium, the site of his regional headquarters, will be engaged in the most intense fighting. The "northern pole alliance" will diminish his power by breaking down his chain of command, communication capabilities, etc. and attempt to break his stranglehold on his conquered territories. This is the beginning of a turning point in WWWIII.

6.12. North Pole Alliance of North America, Europe, Russia forms

(Centurie VIII, Quatrain 17)

At a point the Antichrist's forces become complacent from so many frequent and rapid conquests. They will begin to lose some battles and see their power is not forever.

The Antichrist will have taken over a large part of the world and will become complacent. "Three brothers", the "alliance of the pole", i.e. North America, Europe, and Russia, will trouble the Antichrist and his world will tremble. France will be united with the alliance in spirit, if not actually physically, because the country will weaken seriously from the Antichrist's degradations.

6.13. Ogmios confronts the Antichrist, fate of world in balance

(Centurie V, Quatrain 80)

A leader figuratively referred to as "Ogmios" will confront the Antichrist in battle. The crux of the pivotal struggle of WWWIII will be in the "gray area" between Europe and Asia. The outcome will be questionable for some time. During the time the Antichrist is in power there will be constant skirmishes and battles between his barbarian forces and those still free of his tyrannical rule.

(Centurie II, Quatrain 85)

Ogmios will eventually emerge triumphantly victorious over the Antichrist, but it will be a long, gradual, arduous struggle.

6.14. Antichrist eventually dethroned

(Centurie IX, Quatrain 73)

The Antichrist will rule for "less than the revolution of Saturn" (29.5 years), far less than the grand span of time he envisions. His reign will be temporary, because his power is like building a fire with grass; it burns very hotly but quickly. His effect on history and his "time in the limelight" will be limited. The time from WWII to the end of WWWIII and the time of troubles will almost encompass a century in itself. =

Part VII: The geological and spiritual earth shift

7.1. Timing

Earthquakes and volcanic eruptions are due to the activity caused by the conjunction of the planets, which also affects the shift of this planet A shift will occur at the close of the century. It will be abrupt as to be within a "six to ten-hour period".

7.2. The end of civilization

Civilization as you know it will cease to exist Cities will no longer exist as we know them

7.3. Geography

Continents as you know them now will cease to exist or change dramatically All the central part of your continent as you know it will be [spared]. Continents all over the earth will be affected. The water mass as we know it now will cover a greater percentage of the earth. Continents that are connected will be split, divided by water that was not divided by water before. There will not be any country that is not affected. A large portion of Asia will be covered with water. Africa will have a channel cutting through it, a new strait

7.4. Preparations/Survival

Make humanity aware. Let people prepare themselves spiritually. Intellectually become more aware of survival through climactic changes Problems of survival will be hardest in countries turned into islands

7.5. Old vs. Young Souls

There is now a higher proportion of old souls in the world than there has ever been before, because the old souls will be needed to help the world survive. They can be found everywhere, permeated in the oddest places. The old souls will be in communication with each other and they are the ones that will help things hold together and survive.

Nostradamus states that his communication is intended to help us avoid the worst-case scenarios of his visions that could be averted with great determination and resolve. The time of troubles will be a very trying time. The spirits on the earth at this time are there by choice to work through major amounts of karma. Living in this stressful period will be like concentrated karma, or the equivalent of ten average human lifetimes.

The older and more advanced spirits volunteered. Some younger spirits were simply feeling adventurous. Others are here not because they wanted to in their hearts, but they had to or it would be the "end of the line for them" as far as spiritual advancement. They're not fully volunteers but just enforced volunteers, so to speak, because they knew they had no other choice. Most of the people are understandably unhappy, but some make the best of the situation and some don't.

7.6. The New Age of spiritual rebirth

The shift will usher the beginning of a new age Even though there will be physical deaths; there is no death of people's consciousness, but a different awareness. Do not feel that people would not know life. There will be those that will be left here to make a new beginning for the earth

Whether the worst of the events prophesied come to pass, there will be a great spiritual rebirth throughout the world. Individuals will have the opportunities to "get in touch with themselves" and come to a realization about the falsehoods of materialism. After communication is restored after the time of troubles, people will come to this realization together, and a great rebirth of philosophy that blends the Eastern and Western religions will ensue.

It will be a worldwide movement upholding the Truth as everyone perceives it, bringing about the best aspects of the Age of Aquarius. Focusing on this "ray of hope" during the time of troubles could alleviate the worst aspects of the suffering; the materialism of the majority of the population will regrettably make this unlikely.

7.7. Reawakening of freedoms an rights

(Centurie II, Quatrain 44)

The U.S. will suffer defeats fighting the Antichrist as well as an internal political deterioration during the time of troubles. When the time of troubles are over people will celebrate their victory and freedom, and reawaken in the U.S. the spirit of liberty and rights embodied by the Statue of Liberty, which were dead during the time of the Antichrist's tyranny. The people will regain their rights and the way of life will improve from the dark times.

7.8. Peace after WWWIII

(Centurie VI, Quatrain 24)

An American president with a strong Cancer influence will push for war and cause events to fall in place for it. But after WWWIII the populace will be repulsed by war and elect a new president. He will want peace and work for it, and peace will reign for some time afterwards.

7.9. Spirituality transcends technology

(Centurie IV, Quatrain 29)

This quatrain refers to the grand design that is emanating from the "center of the wheel" during the time of troubles and the healing period afterwards. The sun and Mercury/Hermes are symbols of "the higher aspects". The sun in this quatrain represents the overall power of the universe from which everything originates. Mercury represents the materialistic aspects of technology. Hermes, in relation with Mercury, symbolizes modern communications technology. Vulcan, i.e. one who works with fire, represents warfare.

The "hidden sun" represents the fact that the societies of the world have gotten out of touch with their spiritual source. They are ignorant of their origin and the "meaning of life" and they search for fulfillment and happiness in other areas, and do not succeed. They think it's found in modern technology, hence the "sun being eclipsed by Mercury". It's held only second because what people really hold first is personal pleasure and happiness. And in trying to find happiness in technology they separate themselves from the central source of the universe.

By the end of WWWIII and the time of troubles, and the healing process begins, people will be reunited with the source. The horrors of war and bloodshed--the powers of Vulcan--will cause them to realize that technology does not contain the answers to happiness. They will gain a new insight into "from whence they sprang and where they are going". The time of healing will usher a more spiritually mature age, and people will be able to heal themselves and the world, and go far in preparing to join the community of the Watchers.

The central hub of the "wheel" represents the source of everything and radiating spokes symbolize channels of power. The space between the spokes contains different scenes in the background, representing the various influences the "aspects" have on historical developments as a result of the intensity of the associated energies.

7.10. Feminine aspects of God revered again

(Centurie II, Quatrain 87)

The feminine aspects of God have been ignored, neglected and reviled. After the demise of the Antichrist the pendulum will swing back into balance. In early ages and in ancient societies the female aspect of God was worshipped and revered. The masculine aspect was also respected but was subordinate. During the patriarchal era, which extends into the present, the female aspect was suppressed and repressed. Society will come to terms with the divinity of both masculine and feminine aspects. This realization will help foster a more balanced worldview.

7.11. More open, frequent contact with extraterrestrials

(Centurie I, Quatrain 29)

After the time of troubles there will be much closer and open contact with extraterrestrials and UFOs. One extraterrestrial race will be heading for an undersea, seafloor base they have established but the craft will malfunction and be cast up on the shore. The people will perceive them as the enemy out of terror. Some of the "Others" are enemies, and some are not. There is more than one group of "Watchers". Some mean well for mankind and some have more selfish motives in mind.

7.12. "Green" revolution, return to the land

(Centurie II, Quatrain 19)

People will turn to peace after the horrors of the Antichrist. A "green" revolution with roots in the social revolution of the early 0s will ensue. People will live in extended families beyond the nuclear families of the modern era. Larger families and groups of people are needed to build and support new communities. The new communities will be very earth and ecology-conscious. They will help heal the earth of the horrible degradations of weaponry from WWWIII.

They will reclaim and cultivate wasted, misused, or unusable land for farmland. Since the will for peace is all-encompassing, building defenses will not be necessary. In direct reversal of the 20th century trend, cities will be torn down to expose soil to sunlight and make room for farming. So many will have died during WWWIII that plenty of land will be available to the low-density population. People will be inherently pacific and reclaim land beneath concrete instead of fighting over land.

7.13. New political alliances

(Centurie II, Quatrain 22)

After the calamitous events of the late 20th century, the present alliances among the countries, particularly western nations, will dissolve and new alignments will form. During the interim period the people involved with the peace-keeping system beneath the existing alliance will be "at loose ends". A secret naval or intelligence base will be constructed on the American continental shelf underneath the ocean for secrecy. Heads of staff will meet there to decide what action to take in regard to the new alliance. NATO will not be known by this name but will live on in a similar organization that stemmed from it. This will be dissolved due to the stress countries underwent during the time of troubles.

7.14. Scientific discoveries reaffirm Eastern religion

(Centurie II, Quatrain 22)

Military scientists--not those researching weapons, but doing research-- will discover a new force other than the basic ones of electricity, magnetism, gravity, etc. shortly after the time of troubles. This new force will give supporting evidence for Eastern religious views. The countries in this part of the world, particularly India, will "turn inward" to contemplate the discovery and rise in greater glory than through outward communication with other nations. It is not so much a discovery but a realization.

The evidence for the force has been in front of us but the facts have been misinterpreted and wrongly associated with other phenomena, such as "statistical aberration". The force will relate to mystical phenomena such as teleportation.

7.15. Great Genius unifies religion and science

(Centurie VII, Quatrain 14)

The Great Genius will help unify science and religion and bring about the enlightenment and peace of the Age of Aquarius foretold by prophets. People will be able to free their inner selves and open themselves up to the higher powers and the higher levels of the universe. In effect it will make everyone a philosopher. Sects and religions that embrace the newly discovered principles will be widespread as adherents meet and share experiences in exploring the "upper regions".

7.16. Great Genius discovers the science of miracles

(Centurie III, Quatrain 2)

The great genius will realize the magic of alchemy through his discoveries and inventions. The new philosophy engendered by his discoveries will encourage the development of mental powers and anything will seem possible in the climate of a greater unity of mind, soul, body, and emotions. People will be able to manipulate the basic forces of the universe in a way that will seem utterly fantastic to those not involved with the occult. People presently involved in occult and psychic realms currently deal with these forces without understanding, but in the future understanding will be present, sharpening the efficacy of the art.

7.17. Astonishing feats of medicine

(Centurie II, Quatrain 13)

Future medicine will reach astonishing sophistication by today's standards and will eventually be able to renew a body or "breathe back the spirit" into, i.e. reanimate the body. A breakthrough in science will have a profound effect and man will finally "touch God", so to speak. The spiritual core of the universe that animates everything through life-force will be discovered, the central source of this the divine spirit. It will seem like a profound rebirth of humanity.

7.18. New philosophy of the Age of Aquarius

(Centurie I, Quatrain 69)

A new philosophy will emerge in the New Age, more compatible with the reality of the higher planes and life on earth. The philosophy will have seven basic tenets that appear simple on the surface but are actually very deep. After a period of peace the people of earth will become lax and uncaring of the higher aspects of spirituality because they "have it easy". A war and famine and other hardships will turn minds toward higher realizations as people think there must be something more to their existence. It will absolve existing contradictions in philosophies that perplex people, and will overturn older, established religions. It will have sociological effects and will affect the laws of countries. The philosophy has its roots in the Age of Aquarius.

Part VIII: The Great Genius

8.1. Past events

These are quatrains that refer to past events. I am including them here to give the reader a way to judge Nostradamus' credibility in prophesying. Note that Nostradamus dealt especially with calamitous world events like WWI and WWII, and areas of personal interest, e.g. the French Revolution or advances in science and medicine.

Discovery of microorganisms by Pasteur (Centurie I, Quatrain 25) WWI and WII, atomic bombing (Centurie III, Quatrain 75) radiation from atomic bombing (Centurie V, Quatrain 8) Hitler's fall and suicide, backlash against Nazism (Centurie III, Quatrain 36) Japanese and German imperialism in WWII, atomic bomb (Centurie IV, Quatrain 95) Nixon's diplomacy with China (Centurie II, Quatrain 89) Cold war and the Cuban Missile Crisis (Centurie V, Quatrain 78) Microchips, electronics/communication revolution (Centurie III, Quatrain 13) Challenger shuttle disaster, NASA politics (Centurie VI, Quatrain 34) Misuse of Presidential office in Watergate (Centurie VII, Quatrain 41) Abuse of power by unsavory fundamentalist leaders (Centurie II, Quatrain 27) Rise of AIDS (Centurie II, Quatrain 53)

8.2. Cover-ups

These are some quatrains that refer to current or past situations but are not part of recorded history due to the cover-ups. If evidence of these came to light it would certainly be outstanding evidence of Nostradamus' capabilities for seeing the truth.

Secret Russian voyage to Venus (Centurie IV, Quatrain 28)

-- The Russians sent a manned mission to Venus as a way of competing with the American mission to the Moon. The astronauts died.

-- Secret Viet Nam involvement and POW's (Centurie II, Quatrain 89)

The U.S. is covertly involved in manipulating Viet Nam political structure and actual American prisoners are being held, not necessarily from the war, but from the secret involvement.

8.3. Incidents

These are miscellaneous events predicted for our times.

-- Discovery of extraterrestrial meteorite/ore .(Centurie I, Quatrain 21)

Somewhere in western North America a meteorite will be found by miners looking for ore. They think it might be radioactive but it is a useful new element on the periodical table.

-- Tomb of ancient influential Roman philosopher discovered (Centurie III, Quatrain 65)

The tomb of an ancient Roman figure will be discovered. The man is famous for his philosophy and theories about everything, and his discourses and writings on the nature of things, which are still in existence, and have had a profound effect on Western thought.

8.4. Atlantis

Atlantean civilization existed and the people could work stone with energies the way modern man uses concrete or metal. Physical evidence of Atlantis is spread around the world; one site of the civilization was in the Atlantic on a now-submerged island. The civilization was destroyed when the earth plunged through an asteroid field, either through accident or the deliberate intent of extraterrestrials who felt "threatened" by advancing civilization.

8.5. The Great Genius

The Genius will come the second generation after the Antichrist when people of child-bearing age today have grandchildren, in the mid-21st century

- Great Genius builds space stations and successful artificial intelligence machine, transferring his consciousness to it. Intelligent machines used to manage space stations. Occurs in 21st or 22nd centuries(Centurie IV, Quatrain 32)

- During the time of the Great Genius L-5 space stations will be developed for manufacturing materials in space. Scientific base possibly established on Mars, scientific and communications facility established on the moon. The station will be built negligently. New ways of collecting and distributing solar energy will be devised. (Centurie IX, Quatrain 65)

- The Great Genius will unify religion and science and explain ancient documents, making clear the metaphysical connections between the universe and spirituality. (Centurie VII, Quatrain 14)

- Discovery several centuries after the Great Genius intermeshes grandly with his knowledge and allows people to burst free from all physical bounds and limitations. (Centurie III, Quatrain 94)

8.6. Far Future

(Centurie IV, Quatrain 25)

Mankind will begin to focus on developing himself spiritually. The knowledge for the task has been in front of him but has not been noticed or understood. When he begins to realize what is possible it will astound him.

In the far future interstellar space travel will take place by mind emanations and psychological power, rather than mechanical means.

(Centurie I, Quatrain 17)

Long after the time of the Antichrist and the time of troubles a "forty-cycle" drought will come about. People will survive only by extracting water by melting ice at the poles and distilling it from sea water. Later, the climate will become very wet and copious flooding will occur. This is a natural cycle of the earth, and it causes civilizations to perish during ice ages. "Forty cycles" is something like four thousand years. Man will cause the problems because some aspect of his technology will be endangering the delicate balance of the ecosystem enough to eventually trigger an ice age.

(Centurie X, Quatrain 74)

The "end of the world" will arrive after the seventh cycle which we are currently living in. After this cycle is complete, man's accomplishments on Earth will generally be complete, and even though the Earth will exist for some time forward, the wheel of karma will no longer send man to earth but to other locations.

Human civilization will have fallen down and been rebuilt several times. Some of the old traditions of e.g. bloody, violent gladiatorial games will be passed down through the times into the far future.

(Centurie I, Quatrain 48)

If man can avert the wars, an extensive and peaceful space expansion and exploration can take place, with times of growth and prosperity for humanity. A base will be established on the moon, a major center of communications and scientific research. The base's major purpose is to develop freestanding or self-sufficient space stations in various shapes. All have solar sails that provide energy. This will last for up to 1000 years.

The sun in our solar system will eventually explode in one last burst of energy and then die down to nothing. This will totally incinerate the planet, although the earth will have long since been dead.

Bonus Chapter:

Are You Prepared For World War Three?

When that defining moment finally comes, will you have the time to remember what you could have done to stop it?

Let's pretend, just for the moment, that this is a hypothetical question.

Let's pretend, just for argument's sake, in the comfort of your own easy chair, in front of your own big screen TV, just a few easy steps away from your favorite, anxiety-reducing snacks in your refrigerator, that this is just an academic exercise in geopolitical and psychological speculation, a polite brainstorming session that imaginary participants might conduct if certain coincidental worst case scenarios were to come to pass ... all at the same time.

And let us acknowledge, in the calm certainty of our own typically secure routines, that any resemblance of this imaginary debate to actual persons and events living or dead may not be purely coincidental.

OK? Got it? Pretend it's hypothetical. Just for fun. Then let's begin.

Are you ready for World War Three?

What kind of pathetic paranoid poppycock is that? What IS this? Another

Y2K drill? Much ado about nothing, I think.

Remember. You're pretending it's hypothetical. You agreed.
Oh, all right. Let's see. Mmmmmm .... of course I'm not ready.
Nobody is ready for World War Three. You CAN'T get ready for that.

What will you do when it happens?

Sit here and be vaporized, I guess. What could anybody do?

So ... does that mean you're not ready?

Of course I'm not ready for World War Three! Is anybody ready for World War Three?

Yes, I think there are some people who are ready?

Oh yeah? Who?

Well, three types of groups, at least. First, there are the people who are already victims of major wars, the people in Palestine, Iraq, Afghanistan, Serbia, Colombia, not to mention Burma, the Philippines, Sudan, Zimbabwe, Congo, and certain other countries, people who are already scavenging in often-radioactive garbage dumps just to make ends meet; many of their relatives or children have already been killed by invaders, and they're just living hand to mouth, not caring whether the food they eat or the things they find might be radioactive or not, because when your expected life span is only a few more weeks or months, you don't much care about those things. Survival becomes a day-by-day operation. If the superpowers who have these weapons destroy themselves by using them, that would be good news for the folks routinely diving in dumpsters.

Second, there are the people who plan and wish to execute nuclear wars.

They have already built themselves secure bunkers miles beneath the earth's surface. There are many in the U.S. and Europe. The figure they can ride it out, and they have a new, secret technology that actually detoxifies radioactive contamination, but they're keeping it under wraps until after the
Big One so then they can come out when the coast is clear and continue making scads of money doing two things: cleaning up radioactive rubble and repossessing real estate whose owners have been obliterated, are slowly and agonizingly died of radiation poisoning, or simply have scampered off to more hospitable climes.

Third, there are the people who saw it coming and had the foresight to move to remote locations in the Southern Hemisphere. As long as widespread nuclear explosions didn't trigger a pole shift, those in the lower Southern Hemisphere would be relatively safe from the nuclear winter that will follow World War Three and render the entire Northern Hemisphere completely uninhabitable. The winds in the world are pretty much hemisphere specific, so that the winds that blow around the world in the Northern Hemisphere don't cross over into the southern, and vice versa, although with the magnitude and volume of these explosions in all-out nuclear war, there is bound to be some crossover. Humph. Sonofagun. You have this all worked out, don't you?

What will you do when it actually happens?

When what actually happens?

When World War Three actually happens, how will I find out about it?

Well, there are several ways you could find out about it. If you lived in an urban area like New York or Beijing or Cairo or Teheran, you'd probably find out about it when you saw a flash of light brighter than anything you've ever imagined, but it would last for only a millisecond and then you'd see nothing ever again. If, like most people, you lived in towns moderately close to these cities, you'd probably feel these humongous thumps and wonder why your house was disintegrating all around you. If you lived way out in the sticks you'd start to see these radiant atmospheric flashes, feel relatively gentle ground tremors, and then in a few hours you'd see a smoky blackness creeping toward you from the direction of the cities that would grow blacker and blacker as the hours passed. Depending on each person's individual perceptual skills, it would be a matter of minutes or hours before you realized you would never see the sun again, because you will never survive the abject cold that would be produced by the sun being blotted out for probably from five to 15 years, except, as I said before, in extremely lucky places in the way Southern Hemisphere. Didn't you ever wonder why all those Israelis are buying up huge chunks of real estate in Patagonia?

You mean I won't see something on television and be able to briefly feel a pang of remorse about someone else being killed far away, and then be able to put it out of my mind so I could watch Monday Night Football with my usual intense focus?

Not likely. Here's a variation on the initial question. What would you do if you got information that you really believed and trusted that World War Three was about to start in a few months? What steps would you take to prepare yourself?

How would I know I could trust the information?

82

Well, you'd hear it from the sources you always trusted. Your newspapers, your TV, maybe even from some particularly reliable Internet site.

But would I believe it? Would I be willing to give up everything I've worked for all my life, and just bolt into the wild blue yonder because I read something some journalist, no matter how well connected, might have just dreamed up?

Well, let's say you had an inside source in the secret government, and he told you about the plan. Let's say you regarded it as having the authenticity of all those insider stock tips he'd given you over the years that had made you a bundle. Someone who could discourse effortlessly on Masonic kingpin Albert Pike's 1 prediction that there would be THREE World
Wars and final one would begin in the Middle East and erase both Zionized Christendom and Islamic world in one mighty stroke. And someone who had scary connections with alphabet intelligence agencies.

Yes, I see. What would I do? Hmmm.

Would you run, or would you try to alert others?

Oh dogbiscuits! You know what it's like to tell people that you really know what's going on, and that they don't. They think you've got marbles rattling around in your brain, and they just ignore you, at best. At worst, they call Homeland Security and the men in the little white coats with the large guns show up at your door. At least, you become socially ostracized for not going along with what everybody else believes.

So which would you do?

Well, I guess I'd try to find out if the tip was real or not, and if I determined it WAS real, I'd try to alert the most important people I know to see if they could do something about it.

What would make you decide if the tip was real or not?

Well, our best sources are on TV, I think. At least that's what everybody believes. Most people don't believe something is really real unless they see it on television.

So you're saying that what you see on TV is actually real?

No, I'm not that naive. I know stuff that appears on the news is often shaded by those who own the TV networks to inflict the spin they want to put on most world events. Hell, that's how we got in all those wars.

So what if someone on TV, highly reputable, came on and predicted all-out nuclear war? Would you act on that?

Probably not. I wouldn't believe him.

OK, say you were certain of the tip you received being real. Then what would you do?

I'd call the police, then my congressperson.

And what would you do if they all said you were nuts? And then they said they knew who the bad guys really were, because they had this evidence that they couldn't really tell you about because of National Security, but they were going to nuke them all to smithereens.

I don't know. Cry? Or run into the street screaming.

OK, one more question. If you had the power to impact a large number of people and the money to arrange some effective plan of action to the catch the people who were planning to use nuclear weapons, and you were certain that they were going to carry out their plan on the basis of at least 50 years of continuing

84

atrocities perpetrated against innocent people which they later blamed on completely innocent patsies, what would you do .....?